QUIET MOMENTS
of
Hope
for
MOMS

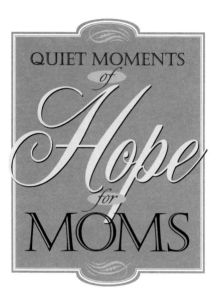

QUIET MOMENTS
of
Hope
for
MOMS

Ellen Banks Elwell

CROSSWAY BOOKS • WHEATON, ILLINOIS
A DIVISION OF GOOD NEWS PUBLISHERS

Published by Crossway Books
　　　　　　A division of Good News Publishers
　　　　　　1300 Crescent Street
　　　　　　Wheaton, Illinois 60187

Cover and Interior designed by: Design Point Inc.

First printing, 1999

Printed in the United States of America

ISBN 0-58134-127-X

Library of Congress Cataloging-in-Publication Data

Elwell, Ellen Banks, 1952-
　　　Quiet moments of hope for moms / Ellen Banks Elwell.
　　　　　　p.　　cm.
　　　Includes bibliographical references.
　　　ISBN 1-58134-127-X (hardcover : alk. paper)
　　　1. Mothers Prayer-books and devotions—English.　2. Devotional
calendars. I. Title.
BV4847.E58　1999
242'.6431—dc21　　　　　　　　　　　　　　　　　99-23366
　　　　　　　　　　　　　　　　　　　　　　　　　　　　　CIP

15	14	13	12	11	10	09	08	07	06	05	04	03	02	01	00	99
15	14	13	12	11	10	9	8	7	6	5	4	3	2	1		

To

Ruthie Howard,

An encouraging friend who
understands reality and promotes hope

Contents

Introduction

One afternoon many years ago the famous artist who painted the ceiling of the Sistine Chapel climbed down from his scaffolding where he had been creating what we now know to be a masterpiece. After eating supper alone, Michelangelo wrote a sonnet to his aching body, the last line of which I find absolutely astounding: "I am no painter."

To think that Michelangelo questioned his effectiveness as a painter gives us comfort when we sometimes question our effectiveness as moms. Hope is what prompted Michelangelo to climb back up the scaffolding each day and continue working on one of the greatest paintings of all time, and hope is what prompts us to face each new day of motherhood (or any other role) with renewed energy and vision.

Every mom needs hope. Hope keeps us going while we're waiting for something very important. Hope sustains us when we don't understand a painful turn of events in our life or the lives of people close to us. Hope prompts us to pray for our child's choices, needs, and relationship with God. Hope that is limited to ourselves, our circumstances, or other people may sometimes feel like no hope at all. But hope that is placed in God, the anchor for our souls' deep needs, is hope correctly focused.

Quiet Moments of Hope for Moms includes five devotional readings per week, all related to a weekly topic, with suggested Bible readings for weekends or extra days. Some readings address the mother-child relationship directly, while others focus on the growth of our souls as Christian women. Each daily reading begins with a Bible verse or verses and ends with a short prayer, encouraging us to extend our thanks, confessions, needs, and praise to God, who loves us deeply and wants us to spend time with Him.

My hope is that in this book we will find truth, encouragement, and direction. May it promote hope on days that don't feel very hopeful from our limited human perspective, and may it point always to Christ, who is the Source of our hope.

Ellen Banks Elwell, 1999

1

Hope

ONE

Hope

We wait in hope for the LORD; he is our help and our shield. In him our hearts rejoice, for we trust in his holy name. May your unfailing love rest upon us, O LORD, even as we put our hope in you.
PSALM 33:20-22

Have you ever waited for something very important? For a parent to come to Christ? For a child to complete cancer treatments? For a husband who has strayed from God's truth to return? Waiting is so hard. Joseph, a Bible character in the Old Testament, spent a fair amount of his life waiting. I've often wondered what his life must have been like—first in the dry well where his brothers dumped him, and then as he waited again before he was sold in Egypt to Potiphar, one of Pharaoh's officials. But the Bible tells us that God was with Joseph and that Joseph experienced success in all that he did.

Even when falsely accused and sent to prison, Joseph knew God showed him extra kindness through the prison warden. After two more years of waiting, Joseph was not only called out of prison to interpret Pharaoh's dream, but he was put in charge of Pharaoh's palace and ultimately the whole land of Egypt. Not even knowing there was still something to wait for, Joseph was eventually reunited with his family in a miraculous way that only God could have arranged!

Was Joseph waiting on his brothers? The Ishmaelites? Potiphar? The cupbearer? Yes, but he was also waiting on God. The influence and possibly even forgetfulness of some of those individuals were all part of God's larger plan for the world. Are you experiencing a time of waiting in your life? Remember, we're not only waiting on people or a process—we're waiting on God.

God who sees and provides,
May I experience Your unfailing love as I put my hope in You. Amen.

Hope

or everything that was written in the past was written to teach us,
so that through endurance and the encouragement of the
Scriptures we might have hope.
ROMANS 15:4

I once had a part-time job playing violin for services at a funeral home. I sat through many sermons from a variety of religious perspectives. Some messages were downright depressing, but the ones I appreciated were talks that contained words of hope. Not hollow, fluffy words, but words that came from God's Word. God's Word consistently gives us encouragement that lasts.

Based on Romans 15:4, I believe that a large part of our hope comes from the *encouragement* of God's Word. Sometimes we read it ourselves, other times we hear God's Word taught at church or a Bible study, and hopefully our friends encourage us with it from time to time. Not long ago I was feeling in a panic after receiving some bad news, but when I opened my Bible to Psalm 94:19 and read, "LORD, when doubts fill my mind, when my heart is in turmoil, quiet me and give me renewed hope and cheer" (TLB), I was encouraged.

Endurance is the other aspect of hope mentioned in Romans 15:4. God graciously gives us choices, and one of our choices is endurance, as opposed to giving up. Endurance is the act, power, or quality of carrying on despite hardships or difficulties. We can give our children lots of encouragement on their homework, but unless they choose to *do* it—to endure—they have no hope of doing well. Hope is like that for us too. We receive encouragement from God's Word, but we must also choose to carry on!

Father,
Thank You for the encouragement we receive from Your Word. May we choose to endure with Your help and strength. Amen.

THREE

Hope

"For nothing is impossible with God."
LUKE 1:37

The angel's announcement of the virgin birth had the word *impossible* written all over it. Mary wasn't married, she hadn't experienced sexual relations, and she was probably no older than fourteen. Furthermore, Nazareth, Mary's hometown, was an unlikely location for an important proclamation such as this. Not even mentioned in the Old Testament, Nazareth was despised by the people in Judah.

When the angel Gabriel visited Mary, he gave her a lot of information in a short amount of time. He told her that she was favored by God, that God was with her, that she would give birth to a son, and that she should name Him Jesus. This would not be just any son—He would be the Son of God, and His kingdom would never end!

Mary's response is a pattern for us. She didn't say, "This is impossible!" She said, "How will this be?" In other words, how will this be possible? She understood what would happen, but she didn't understand *how* it would happen.

Are you facing an impossible situation? Do circumstances seem hopeless or insurmountable? Examine the angel's answer to Mary. The angel announced that the Holy Spirit would overshadow her, and she would experience the transforming power of God's presence. He encouraged her with news that Elizabeth, her very old cousin, was also pregnant—another seeming impossibility, reminding her that with God nothing is impossible.

As believers, we too have the presence of God's Spirit who specializes in transforming and encouraging our hearts. May we, like Mary, ask "How?" and submit to God's transforming power in our lives.

Father,
Forgive us for too often responding to difficulties with "This is impossible!" instead of looking to You and asking, "How, God?" Thanks for Your Spirit who teaches and encourages us. Amen.

And if I go and prepare a place for you, I will come back and take you to be with me that you also may be where I am."
JOHN 14:3

Peter Marshall knew a mom whose son was critically ill and facing death. The mother had spent hours nursing him and playing with him, knowing that the boy's days on earth were short. One day the boy asked his mother what it would be like to die. After the mother prayed for wisdom and composure, she said, "Kenneth, do you remember when you were a tiny boy how you used to play so hard all day that when night came you were too tired even to undress and you'd tumble into your mother's bed and fall asleep? That was not your bed, it was not where you belonged. You would only stay there a little while. Much to your surprise you would wake up and find yourself in your own bed in your own room. You were there because someone had loved you and taken care of you. Your father had come with big strong arms and carried you away. Kenneth, darling, death is just like that. We just wake up some morning to find ourselves in the other room. Our room where we belong, because the Lord Jesus loved us and died for us."

The lad's shining face looking up into hers told her that the point had gone home and there would be no more fear, only love and trust in his little heart as he went to meet the Father in heaven. He never questioned again. Several weeks later he fell asleep just as she had said, and his Father's big, strong arms carried him to his own room.

Father,
Thank You that Your hope and peace come to the hearts of believers of all ages as they trust in You. Amen.

FIVE

Hope

or I know the plans I have for you, says the Lord. They are plans for good and not for evil, to give you a future and a hope.

JEREMIAH 29:11, TLB

I just received a royalty check from Hope Publishing Company yesterday. The name of the company holds extra meaning to me because of hope God brought to me during an especially difficult time of my life.

My early thirties included some cloudy times of sadness and depression. Without recounting some of the surrounding events, it's enough to say that I was feeling insignificant, and my life seemed to have lost its joy. One day a friend sent an encouraging note in the mail, ending with the verse written above.

Several months later I received a phone call from the senior editor of Hope Publishing, saying their company wanted to publish a new series of praise books for student pianists, and asking if I'd be interested in compiling and arranging one book. I was flattered, but my response was, "I've never done that before." To which the editor said, "Send us two arrangements and let us decide."

I did my best, sent in the arrangements, and waited. About a month later an envelope came from Hope Publishing. I thought, *Here's my "Thanks but no thanks" letter.* I was shocked when I found a letter saying, "Here's the contract. Would you please do a whole book?" I still remember sitting down on the couch, having a good cry, and thanking God for blessing me with a huge affirmation of hope. The experience demonstrated to me that God cares about me.

Father,
Thanks for providing bright rays of hope at times when our lives seem overcast with dark clouds. Thank You that You are the God of hope. Amen.

EXTRA READINGS FOR DAYS 6 AND 7
Psalm 33; Romans 15:1-13

2

Prayer

ONE

Prayer

*She was in deep anguish and was crying bitterly
as she prayed to the Lord.*
1 SAMUEL 1:10, TLB

Have you ever experienced times of grief, bitterness, or anguish, when you felt as though you were slipping? Hannah did. Back in the Old Testament book of 1 Samuel (1:1–2:21), we learn that Hannah was one of the wives of Elkanah, a Levite priest. The other wife was Peninnah. Each year the combined families made a trip to the Shiloh tabernacle, and each year the same thing happened: Elkanah celebrated his sacrifices by giving gifts to Peninnah and each of her children, but Hannah received only one for herself because she had no children. The Bible tells us that Peninnah laughed at Hannah's barrenness, making Hannah cry so much that she couldn't eat.

One evening in Shiloh, Hannah went over to the temple. Out of her bitter grief and anguish, she cried out to the Lord. In the process of praying, she endured even *more* taunting, because the priest mistook her grief feelings for drunkenness! But something amazing happened after she poured out her heart to God. The priest gave her a blessing of peace, and after she left the temple, she ate and her face was no longer downcast. After worshiping God together, the families went home, and Hannah became pregnant. We find Hannah's beautiful song of praise in 1 Samuel 2:1-10. What's the lesson for us?

In our grief or anguish, we can cry out to God, acknowledging that He is God and we are not. We can pour out our souls—grief, bitterness, and all. And after we bring Him our requests, we can get on with our lives and worship God, thankful that He hears us.

Father,
Thank You for examples of women like Hannah, who experienced some of the same feelings of grief and bitterness we have from time to time. Thank You that we can pour out our hearts to You and that You give us the grace and strength to stand up and get on with our lives. Thanks for Your answers to our prayers. Amen.

Prayer

With this in mind, we constantly pray for you, that our God may count you worthy of his calling, and that by his power he may fulfill every good purpose of yours and every act prompted by your faith.

2 THESSALONIANS 1:11

I just snuck into my son Nathan's bedroom and straightened the blankets over his sleeping body—all six-feet-two of it. He returned home today from a mission trip to Bucharest, Romania, with his church youth group, and it is *so* good to have him home even if he is asleep. During the weeks he was gone, we were able to communicate through E-Mail, and that was great. But I especially appreciated the opportunity to pray for him all through the day, and even sometimes when I woke up at night.

When I communicate with him through letters or E-Mail, I catch up on the news. But when I pray, there's an added dimension to communication. I talk to Nathan's Creator and my Creator, his Savior and my Savior, his sustainer and my sustainer. The God who is everywhere at once and who knows everything knows how much I care for Nathan, and He hears my prayers on his behalf no matter what hour of the day or night.

So whether our children are in our house, down the street, or across the world, we can communicate with God on their behalf, having confidence that God sees their bodies, minds, and hearts. Mark Twain once said, "I don't know of a single foreign product that enters this country untaxed except the answer to prayer." Prayer, unlike long-distance phone calls, does not cost money. We don't have to shop around for the best rates or the best times—we can talk to God anytime!

God who is everywhere and never sleeps,
Thank You that we can pray to You anytime and anywhere on behalf of our children. Thank You that You are the God who sees and provides. Amen.

THREE

Prayer

Pour out your heart like water in the presence of the Lord. Lift up your hands to him for the lives of your children.

LAMENTATIONS 2:19

"One day I returned home from school with one of those infamous notes from my elementary school teacher. I had the 'gift' of talking in class and talking back to my teacher. My mother was becoming more and more frustrated by my behavior at school and her inability to change my attitude.

"On this occasion she stood there with tears in her eyes, and then she led me to her bedroom. I was expecting a well-deserved spanking, but what I got was far more effective. She had me kneel down with her as she prayed and asked the Lord for wisdom to guide her son. And as she prayed, she cried. I was deeply moved. If my behavior was that important to her, I knew I had to change. No spanking I ever received had as much impact as kneeling next to my praying mother."

Dennis Eenigenburg, pastor.[1]

Haven't all of us moms, at some point, become frustrated by the behavior or attitudes of our children, our husbands, or ourselves? The Old Testament book of Lamentations expresses the anguish of the Jewish people over the utter ruin of their city. Although most of us have not lived through the painful experience of having another nation conquer us, we sometimes experience anguish over a rebellious child, a husband we're concerned about, or an area in which we lack self-control in our own lives. Pouring our hearts out to God in these situations is the very *best* thing we can do.

Father,
Like the prophet Jeremiah, may we acknowledge our pain, but call it to mind with hope: "Because of the LORD's great love we are not consumed, for his compassions never fail. They are new every morning; great is your faithfulness." Amen.

FOUR

Prayer

And pray in the Spirit on all occasions with all kinds of prayers and requests. With this in mind, be alert and always keep on praying for all the saints.

EPHESIANS 6:18

This verse is so full of help for us on the habit of prayer that it's exciting to unpack all the instructions!

1. "Pray in the Spirit." At the outset of our prayers, we are wise to ask for the Spirit's help because, as Romans 8:26-27 explains, the Spirit helps us when we don't know how to pray, and even when we think we do.

2. "Pray . . . on all occasions." In *The Christian Mom's Idea Book*, one mom suggested, "I pray at the sink, in the car, in the doctor's waiting room, with joy, with tears, through hardships, for the future, in all aspects and places of life."[2]

3. "Pray . . . with all kinds of prayers." One minute we might be thanking God, and five minutes later we may need to confess something to Him. Sometimes we offer praise, and sometimes it's great to pray Scripture back to God.

4. "Keep on praying." Be persistent. My pastor, Kent Hughes, tells how he prayed for *thirty years* that his brother

would come to Christ, and one day when he was visiting in his brother's den, his brother said to Kent, "Let's talk about my soul." They ended up praying together, and his brother came to Christ!

5. "Praying for all the saints." Our prayers for fellow believers help them overcome the enemy and increase God's kingdom.

Prayer costs us no money, and the lines of communication are never overcrowded. What an incredible privilege it is to pray!

Father,
Thank You that when You teach us that we should pray, You also teach us how to do it effectively. May we do it. Amen.

FIVE

Prayer

How many times each day do I encounter challenges that I could pray about? Often. How much time each day do I actually spend praying? Probably not enough. I'm presently aware of several hot-potato situations that family and friends are experiencing, and these concerns pop into my mind many times throughout each day. What do I learn from God's Word that can help me with these concerns?

It's interesting that the verse above begins with a call to confession. Sin brings great isolation to our lives that produces ugly selfishness for the person perpetuating a sin and unhealthy hiding and protecting for those around the person practicing it.

However we become aware of another's problems, we have the responsibility and privilege to pray. Kent Hughes writes:

There is power in a confessing fellowship, but the power is not in the confessing, as necessary as it is, but in the resulting prayer, as is emphasized by the last half of verse 16: "and pray for each other so that you may be healed. The prayer of a righteous man is powerful and effective."[3]

Practical ways of praying for specific needs are:

- Pray using Scripture (see Psalm 25:8; 86:11; 119:37; 1 Thessalonians 5:23-24; Hebrews 13:20-21; James 3:17).
- Pray at specific times each day.
- Leave post-it notes on the mirror or above the kitchen sink.
- Use time alone in the car to pray.
- Remember that *caring* and *doing* are great, but praying is powerful and effective!

Father,
Thanks for the reminder from Your Word that our prayers can be powerful and effective. Thanks for those who pray for us. May we be faithful to do the same for our family and friends. Amen.

EXTRA READINGS FOR DAYS 6 AND 7
1 Samuel 1:1-20; 1 Kings 18:16-45

3

Prayer

CONTINUED

ONE

Prayer

So Ahab went off to eat and drink, but Elijah climbed to the top of Carmel, bent down to the ground and put his face between his knees.

1 KINGS 18:42

There was a battle going on here, but it wasn't really between Elijah and Ahab—it was between God and Baal. After a three-and-a-half-year drought, God had instructed Elijah to go to Ahab with a message that God would provide rain. After Elijah delivered the message, he challenged 850 prophets of Baal to a contest on Mount Carmel, where each side offered sacrifices to their God without building a fire. The true God would reveal himself by igniting the fire. All the pagan prophets' praying to Baal failed, but when Elijah prayed to the Lord (even with *water* having been poured over his offering), God sent fire from heaven to consume the sacrifice. The people of Israel praised God, and the prophets of Baal were destroyed.

But the rain hadn't come yet. Notice the distinctly different postures of Elijah and Ahab. Ahab went off to eat and drink; Elijah got alone to pray, bending down to the ground with his face between his knees. One partied, and one prayed passionately.

Elijah knew that whenever God asks His people to do something, He doesn't leave them without the resources to carry out the task. We sometimes forget that prayer is our biggest and most powerful resource!

What task do you have in front of you today? Paying the bills? Dealing with a child who has a chronic problem? Whether we need wisdom with finances, raising children, help in forgiving another, or strength to make obedient choices, we are wise to get on our knees and passionately ask for God's help.

God of Elijah, whose name meant "God is my Helper,"
Please be my helper today in the challenges set before me. May I run to You in prayer, realizing that You are my most powerful helper. Amen.

TWO
Prayer

O my people, trust him all the time. Pour out your longings
before him, for he can help!
PSALM 62:8, TLB

What do we do when we're up against a problem that's far bigger than anything we can handle? Some problems in life are solvable—like the time I turned on my blender when the top wasn't *securely* fastened. It made quite a mess in my kitchen, but in ten or fifteen minutes I had it cleaned up. Larger problems that can't be "solved" either quickly or easily—like giving birth to a baby who has severe medical problems—are accompanied by some overwhelming feelings.

I remember a time I encountered a life experience that I neither wanted nor understood. All I knew was that I felt a lot of pain and sadness. I decided to get alone for one day of thinking and praying. I wasn't really alone though. I have special memories of God's presence and strength washing over me as I paced the floor with open Bible in hand, reading accounts of people in the Bible who met up with seemingly impossible circumstances. The common denominator in their prayers was that they thought about things God had done in the past, like parting the waters of the Red Sea and protecting Daniel in the lions' den.

We too are wise to begin our prayers with reminders of things God has done in the past, which helps answer the question we all ask when we hit a snag—"Is God *really* in control?" As we remember what He has done in the past and cry out to Him for help in our present situation, our hearts are stirred to trust Him.

Father,
Thank You for the honesty of the psalmists and other writers in the Bible who were good examples for us of how to pray even when our hearts are heavy. May we rehearse Your faithfulness to us and pour out our longings to You. Amen.

THREE

Prayer

In the same way, the Spirit helps us in our weakness. We do not know what we ought to pray, but the Spirit himself intercedes for us with groans that words cannot express. And he who searches our hearts knows the mind of the Spirit, because the Spirit intercedes for the saints in accordance with God's will.

ROMANS 8:26-27

Have you ever experienced times when you wanted to pray about a very distressing or confusing matter, but you just didn't have the words? There have been times that I was so sad or perplexed that thinking about putting my feelings into words seemed overwhelming. At times like that, it is very comforting to know that God knows us better than we think we know ourselves. Not only does God know *our* thoughts, but *He* has thoughts and intents for us that are entirely right and pure, and that's more than we can say of ourselves.

God is much more interested in the purity of our hearts and thoughts than He is in hearing fancy prayers that come from a corrupt heart. When the words just won't come, groans sometimes feel more appropriate. We aren't the only ones groaning, because the Bible tells us that God's Spirit groans with us, sharing the burdens of our weakness and suffering. But He doesn't stop at groaning — He also prays for us. And His prayer is that we will be led into God's will even in the middle of suffering.

It is encouraging to understand that when I encounter situations in my life that I cannot analyze or pray about intelligently, groaning or pleading for God's help is a very good thing to do. How freeing it is to know that the Spirit's prayers on my behalf are *totally* in agreement with God's plans.

Father,
We thank You that when we pray, You do not evaluate our words but rather our hearts. Even when we can't find the words, Your Spirit is gracious to pray for us. Thank You that You care about us very much. Amen.

FOUR

Prayer

For this reason, since the day we heard about you, we have not stopped praying for you and asking God to fill you with the knowledge of his will through all spiritual wisdom and understanding.

COLOSSIANS 1:9

Mary, one of my friends from church, hosted a prayer time one fall for moms whose children had gone off to college. We enjoyed a wonderful time of praying together for the needs of our children. Something that made it particularly special was that Mary suggested we use Scripture to pray back to God some of the specific ways He wants us all to grow to be more like Him.

I have found this to be helpful not only in my prayers for my children, but also in prayers for my husband, myself, and my friends and extended family. For this section on prayer, I suggest several verses from God's Word that we can pray back to God on behalf of our children. As you spend time in God's Word, I'm sure you will find many more prayer verses. But these are good for a start.

And this is my prayer: that your love may abound more and more in knowledge and depth of insight, so that you may be able to discern what is best and may be pure and blameless until the day of Christ, filled with the fruit of righteousness that comes through Jesus Christ—to the glory and praise of God.

Philippians 1:9-11

Now I commit you to God and to the word of his grace, which can build you up and give you an inheritance among all those who are sanctified.

Acts 20:32

God of the Bible,
Thank You for leaving us Your Word of Truth. Thank You that Your words add power to our prayer. Amen.

FIVE
Prayer

I will try to walk a blameless path, but how I need your help, especially in my own home, where I long to act as I should.

PSALM 101:2, TLB

In yesterday's devotional I suggested some verses from the Bible that a mom might pray back to God for her children. Today I want to focus on verses that we moms might pray for *ourselves.*

> *For God did not give us a spirit of timidity, but a spirit of power, of love, and of self-discipline.*
>
> 2 Timothy 1:7
>
> *If any of you lacks wisdom, he should ask God, who gives generously to all without finding fault, and it will be given to him.*
>
> James 1:5
>
> *I pray that out of his glorious riches he may strengthen you with power through his Spirit in your inner being, so that Christ may dwell in your hearts through faith. And I pray that you, being rooted and established in love, may have power, together with all the saints, to grasp how wide and long and high and deep is the love of Christ, and to know this love that surpasses knowledge—that you may be filled to the measure of all the fullness of God.*
>
> Ephesians 3:16-19

Lord, when doubts fill my mind, when my heart is in turmoil, quiet me and give me renewed hope and cheer.

Psalm 94:19, TLB

Your own soul is nourished when you are kind; it is destroyed when you are cruel.

Proverbs 11:17, TLB

Above all else, guard your affections. For they influence everything else in your life.

Proverbs 4:23, TLB

The Lord will work out his plans for my life—for your lovingkindness, Lord, continues forever. Don't abandon me—for you made me.

Psalm 138:8, TLB

Lord,
Thank You that Your Word is helpful to me as a mom. May I choose to walk down paths that are true and right. Amen.

EXTRA READINGS FOR DAYS 6 AND 7
Colossians 4:2-6; Colossians 1:9-14

4

Security

ONE

Security

Have your kids ever made forts inside or outside your home? My kids have had "forts" at sleepovers made out of blankets duct-taped to tables and chairs. They have also built snow forts. Their largest project was a three-level tree fort in the backyard that took three summers to build.

A "fort" for our kids is a cozy place where they can play, but a fort in the military sense is much more substantial—it's a place of strength and security. God tells us that when we fear Him, *He* is our fortress. Because of God's presence in our lives, the strength and security He provides can be experienced in *any* location.

Corrie ten Boom was a Dutch woman whose parents feared the Lord. During the Nazi invasion of Holland, Corrie's family hid Jewish people in their home so those people wouldn't be sent to the Nazi camps. Sadly, Corrie and her family ended up in those very camps because of their help to the Jews. Corrie's fortress, her refuge in God, was sometimes experienced in the watch shop of her father, sometimes on a train ride, sometimes in the hidden quarters of their home, and sometimes in the bunks of a concentration camp. Her fortress wasn't a physical dwelling. Rather, it was the security of a relationship with God.

We often spend time and money on our actual dwelling places, which is fine. But how much more important that we teach our children to be in awe of God, who is our ultimate security and fortress in all of life, our refuge wherever we may be.

Father,
Thank You that the security we have in You doesn't depend on where we are or where we live. Thank You that we carry it in our souls. Amen.

TWO

Security

*I have set the LORD always before me. Because he is at my right hand,
I will not be shaken. Therefore my heart is glad and my tongue
rejoices; my body also will rest secure.*

PSALM 16:8-9

What mom *doesn't* want to live with assurance and certainty? In my mid-forties, I still have occasional days when I feel insecure. But in my early adult years, I had a lot of those days, and I sometimes thought I was one of very few moms who questioned her worth. Now that I'm twenty years older, I know differently. Every mom who's honest with herself admits that she has some of those days, and sadly, too many moms live a lot of their days there. In order to be a truly secure person, there are two truths from God's Word that we need to keep in balance constantly.

1. It was the awfulness of our personal sin that made the death of Christ necessary.
2. God thought we were worth so much that He sent His Son to *die* for us.

When we concentrate on one and not the other, we get out of balance—we either get too proud or too insecure.

Security begins when we say, like the psalmist in the verses above, "I keep the LORD (not self) always before me."

Our problem with reflecting on self is that our thoughts either lead us to self-praise and self-satisfaction or plunge us into discouragement and despair. . . . God has redeemed us; we can lift up our heads and shout praises. God's love is an in-spite-of kind of love—the kind of love that is safe, that lets us dump our load honestly before him, assured of his constancy.[4]

Now that's a great start toward security!

God,
Thank You that we don't find our sense of security by looking inward to ourselves, but that we start by looking up to You. Thanks that You cared for us so much that You died for us because You wanted us to be your friends forever. Thanks that You are "God with us"! Amen.

THREE

Security

an a mother forget the baby at her breast and have no compassion on the child she has borne? Though she may forget, I will not forget you! See, I have engraved you on the palm of my hands."

ISAIAH 49:15-16

For those of you moms who have nursed children from your breasts, you probably have a picture of security in your mind. I remember times that my babies were oh-so-fussy—either tired, hungry, or just plain old cranky—and the only thing that seemed to satisfy them was putting them to my breast, and they often fell asleep there. Even if there had been a roomful of mothers in the house, *I* was the one who had what the baby needed.

This mental picture of a mother who has power to feed and settle a baby gives us a glimpse into the meaning of El-Shaddai, one of the names of God used in the Old Testament. *El* stands for might or power, and *Shaddai* describes the power of all-bountifulness. *Shaddai* came from the Hebrew word *Shad*, meaning "Breasted."

I need hardly explain how this title, the "Breasted," or the "Pourer-forth," came to mean "Almighty." Mothers at least will understand it. A babe is crying—restless. Nothing can quiet it. Yes! The breast can. A babe is pining—starving. Its life is ebbing away. It cannot take man's proper food; it will die. No. The breast can give it fresh life, nourishment. By her breast the mother has almost infinite power over the child.[5]

In an even more secure and everlasting way, God is our El-Shaddai, the Pourer-forth who pours Himself out for us when we run or cry out to Him.

El-Shaddai,
Milk from mothers' breasts eventually dries up, but your supply of nourishment is everlasting. Thank You that there is always plenty for us all. Amen.

FOUR

Security

Though my father and mother forsake me, the LORD will receive me.
PSALM 27:10

If you were asked to describe a mental picture of the word *security*, what would you describe? I might see a little boy jumping into his father's arms, knowing that his dad would catch him. Or I might envision a mother holding her sleeping baby snugly against her chest. Security is freedom from risk, danger, anxiety, or fear, and we mothers work at providing it for our children.

Sadly, we sometimes hear of parents who do the opposite. I recently heard a news report of a young couple who, after a dispute in their car, left their ten-month-old baby alongside a busy Chicago expressway. Thankfully, a doctor on his way to work saw the baby and took her to the hospital, where she was found to be in good physical condition. At the time of the news report, the state was seeking foster parents for the child.

Again, if you were asked to give a mental picture of *security*, what would it be? I've lived long enough to know that my picture wouldn't be money, a house, a job, a spouse, or health. My picture would have me running into God's arms, knowing that He cares for me even though He has time for everyone else in the world who also wants to spend time with Him. No matter what kind of rejection any of us has experienced, we know that if we come to God, He will *never* forsake us. That's the ultimate in security.

Lord,
Thank You for always being ready to receive us. Thank You that we can run to You at any time about anything, because You are our Creator, and You know us inside out. Thank You that You never forsake us. Amen.

FIVE

Security

For whenever you eat this bread and drink this cup, you proclaim the Lord's death until he comes.

1 CORINTHIANS 11:26

Just about every year my parents invite all four of their children (myself and three siblings) and each of our families to spend a few days together at a local hotel right after Christmas. Each family unit stays in their own suite, and my parents stay in a conference room suite, which ends up being grand central station with lots of food and lots of games! The adults have time to sit around and talk while the kids play games, explore the hotel, and swim in the pool. What a feeling of security and warmth for all of us! The older I get, the more I appreciate my parents' generosity in providing the time for us all to be together.

This morning in a Sunday service at my church, I also experienced great security and warmth as I shared in the Lord's Supper. Along with the rest of the believers in my church family—one little part of the body of Christ, I partook of the bread and wine (grape juice), with the purpose of remembering Christ, receiving strength from Him, and rededicating myself to His purposes.

The Greek word for communion means *fellowship*, *participating*, and *sharing*. What security there is in remembering together that we have been delivered from sin because of Christ's death, and in being reminded again of His presence and power to help us. What anticipation we feel for a day yet to come too when we will experience the *ultimate* in security—sharing communion together with Christ in heaven!

Father,
Thank You for the security of being part of Your family and sharing Communion with other believers, our brothers and sisters in Christ. May we never take it lightly, but always be reminded of Your great love for us and Your great power to help us. Amen.

EXTRA READINGS FOR DAYS 6 AND 7
Psalm 16; Psalm 27

5

Righteousness

ONE

Righteousness

Righteousness exalts a nation, but sin is a disgrace to any people.
PROVERBS 14:34

When calamity comes, the wicked are brought down,
but even in death the righteous have a refuge.
PROVERBS 14:32

The word *righteousness* comes from a root word that means "straightness." Righteousness is upright and holy living that follows God's standards. God is perfectly righteous, and so all righteousness comes from Him. That's why Proverbs 3:5-6 instructs us, "Trust in the LORD with all your heart and lean not on your own understanding; in all your ways acknowledge him, and *he will make your paths straight*" (italics mine).

As we trust in Christ, He shares His righteousness with us, and our character and status as people become elevated. That's how righteousness *exalts* people. Isn't that what all of us want? A raise in character and status! We can't buy this with money, but rather we choose to trust Christ, and He imparts His righteousness to us.

Righteousness not only *exalts* us, but it *protects* us.

People who choose to share the righteousness of Christ find refuge in Him. He is a source of protection, shelter, help, relief, and comfort in times of trouble, hardship, or distress.

> *Trust in him at all times, O people; pour out your hearts to him, for God is our refuge.*
>
> *Psalm 62:8*
>
> *He who dwells in the shelter of the Most High will rest in the shadow of the Almighty. I will say of the LORD, "He is my refuge and my fortress, my God, in whom I trust."*
>
> *Psalm 91:1-2*

Righteousness exalts us, and righteousness protects us, but not because of our own merit. As we trust in Christ, He shares His righteousness with us, and then we are exalted and protected!

Righteous God,
Thank You that because of our relationship with You, we can experience Your righteousness. Thank You that it elevates us and protects us. May we continually trust You so that we will be gracious examples of Your righteousness to those around us. Amen.

TWO

Righteousness

For the LORD watches over the way of the righteous,
but the way of the wicked will perish.

PSALM 1:6

Psalm 1 is rich in word pictures! It invites us to envision a crossroad, two paths, a Bible, a tree, a stream, fruit, green leaves, and garbage blowing in the wind.

The crossroad reminds us that there's a choice for us to make. There are only two paths in life—God's way of righteousness or the way of rebellion and destruction. Which are we on? The pictures of the person who chooses God's way are rich indeed. The person who chooses God's way and spends time in His Word is likened to a tree planted by a river that bears fruit and prospers. This is a picture of something that is growing, lasting, and bringing life to others. This person grows to love the Bible because spending time in God's Word is the way he figures out how to follow God. Meditating means reading and thinking about what we've read, looking to apply it to our lives. The Bible brings us great hope, and the more we know of God's

Word, the more wisdom we'll have to handle the daily decisions of motherhood.

The path of the wicked is not a pretty picture, because it is a picture of garbage. Chaff is an outer shell that has to be removed before getting to the valuable grain inside. After plants were cut and crushed, they were thrown into the air. The chaff blew off as garbage, while the good grain fell to the earth.

We all have a choice to make. Will we choose godliness or garbage?

Father,
Thank You that You promise to bless the person who chooses Your way.
May we choose Your righteous way, not the way of garbage. Amen.

THREE

Righteousness

Let us behave decently, as in the daytime, not in orgies and drunkenness, not in sexual immorality and debauchery, not in dissension and jealousy. Rather, clothe yourselves with the Lord Jesus Christ, and do not think about how to gratify the desires of the sinful nature.

ROMANS 13:13-14

You might ask, "Why would a verse about orgies, drunkenness, sexual immorality, debauchery, dissension, and jealousy be included in this book?" Here's the answer: When people are alienated from God, these behaviors are inevitable.

What is the antidote to the awful behaviors that happen as a result of alienation from God? It's the righteousness of Christ. His righteousness is not something we work hard to attain by doing good things or attempting to get rid of the bad. Rather, try to picture an exchange of clothing; we exchange our filthy garments for a robe of righteousness. Isaiah 61:10 says, "I delight greatly in the LORD; my soul rejoices in my God. For he has clothed me with garments of salvation and arrayed me in a robe of righteousness."

No one can stand in the presence of the Lord God with dirty clothes. The Old Testament ritual of washing clothes and being ready on the third day (Exodus 19:9-11) is a picture of Jesus taking His absolutely sinless life to the cross, paying the redemption price for the sin of His people, and God showing His satisfaction with the payment by triumphantly raising Jesus from the dead on the third day. Then God puts the clothes of Jesus' righteousness on me and declares me to be pure.[6]

Every woman who trusts in Christ exchanges her rags for His righteousness!

Righteous Father,
Thank You that we can be robed with Your righteousness as we trust in You. May we never forget that You paid for our new garment with Your lifeblood. Amen.

Righteousness

o some who were confident of their own righteousness and looked down on everybody else, Jesus told this parable: "Two men went up to the temple to pray, one a Pharisee and the other a tax collector. The Pharisee stood up and prayed about himself: 'God, I thank you that I am not like all other men—robbers, evildoers, adulterers—or even like this tax collector. I fast twice a week and give a tenth of all I get.' But the tax collector stood at a distance. He would not even look up to heaven, but beat his breast and said, 'God, have mercy on me, a sinner.' I tell you that this man, rather than the other, went home justified before God. For everyone who exalts himself will be humbled, and he who humbles himself will be exalted."

LUKE 18:9-14

If we ever get to a time in our life that we feel confident of *our own* righteousness and we look down on other people, we are in a most dangerous place. Jesus addressed the parable in Luke 18:9-14 to that kind of audience, teaching that pride disqualifies us from experiencing the righteousness of God. Only God is the standard for righteousness, because He *is* righteousness.

He is the Rock, his works are perfect, and all his ways are just. A faithful God who does no wrong, upright and just is he.

Deuteronomy 32:4

The contrast Jesus made between the Pharisee and the publican in this parable was *huge*. The Pharisee stood up in the middle of the temple, wanting to be noticed, while the publican stood at a distance, wishing to be out of the way. The Pharisee prayed "about himself," bragging about himself and noting the sins of others, while the tax collector beat on his breast and confessed his own sin. The Pharisee went home unjustified and condemned by his pride, while the publican went home justified and saved by his faith.

Jesus did not take issue with the behavior of the Pharisee—He took issue with the self-righteous attitude of his heart. The lesson here for us is that God desires simplicity, humility, and faith—not fanfare, bragging, and confidence in our self-righteousness. If we exalt ourselves, we will eventually be humbled; but if we humble ourselves before God, we will eventually be exalted.

Father,
Forgive us for taking note of the sins of others instead of confessing our own sins to You. May we daily choose a posture of humility. Amen.

FIVE

Righteousness

The path of the righteous is like the first gleam of dawn, shining ever brighter till the full light of day. But the way of the wicked is like deep darkness; they do not know what makes them stumble.

PROVERBS 4:18-19

In the verses above, we see quite a contrast between the path of the righteous and the way of the wicked. The words "path" and "way" clearly indicate methods of going from one place to another. If I go to Florida, I don't just happen to wake up there one morning. I get there because I made a choice to either fly or drive. The same principle holds true for righteous or wicked living—we make choices that determine which direction we will go.

Righteousness is holy living that conforms to God's standards, impossible for us to attain on our own. Because God is the source of all righteousness, He *is* the standard. The path of righteousness is not hidden. It is well defined, because Christ has already blazed the trail for us. Whenever we spend time with Him through His Word or prayer, and if we choose to obey, we experience the gleam of dawn—an indication that there is more light to come.

The more time a mom spends with Christ, the more she shines, reflecting the light of Christ to her family.

A wicked person is a person who practices sin habitually. "The way of the wicked" is full of darkness because of the absence of light or clarity, and the people on that path are committing sin with regularity. But there is hope—the presence of Jesus can bring righteousness and light to a dark heart that is stumbling for lack of a straight path, because Jesus *is* our righteousness.

Father,
Thank You that the path to righteousness is not a secret, but that Your
righteousness is equally available to all who want You. Amen.

EXTRA READINGS FOR DAYS 6 AND 7
Psalm 1; Romans 13:8-14

6

Grace

ONE

Grace

*Do you think Scripture says without reason that the spirit he caused
to live in us tends toward envy, but he gives us more grace?
That is why Scripture says: "God opposes the proud but gives grace
to the humble." Submit yourselves, then, to God.
Resist the devil, and he will flee from you.*

JAMES 4:5-7

Someone has said, "Man is born broken. He lives by mending. The grace of God is glue." Grace is what we all long for, isn't it? We all long to be shown mercy, love, compassion, and patience. The healthiest people in the world are those who are experiencing the grace of God and are learning to pass it on to others. I guess that also means that the healthiest people in the world are not proud but humble, because proud people don't think they need grace, and they certainly can't pass on to others what they haven't experienced themselves.

The devil is constantly saying to the Christian, "Why keep so closely to the narrow way and the humble path? Why not be more self-assertive? Why not express yourself as fully as you can, and find power and enjoyment in that self-expression? I am the prince of the world and the whole world lies under me. I offer you to the full the pleasures and the happiness of the world." As Christ resisted the evil one, so too must His subjects; and we are assured here that our very resistance will constitute our victory. We can resist because we have been born again as children of God and have the weapon of faith as our shield (see Ephesians 6:16).[7]

And so we see that the path to grace is through faith in Christ that resists the devil, because in that faith we humble ourselves, and grace can only come to the humble.

Father,
We ask forgiveness for our pride. May we daily submit ourselves to You and resist the devil. Thank You for Your grace. Amen.

TWO

Grace

For it is by grace you have been saved, through faith—and this not from yourselves, it is the gift of God.

EPHESIANS 2:8-9

Grace is the favor and kindness of God shown to us in spite of the fact that we don't deserve it. Grace cannot be purchased or earned, because it is a *gift*. But like any gift, it can't be appreciated or experienced unless it is accepted. When we accept God's grace by faith, we become victorious, generous, courteous, and strong.

We are *victorious* because we have already been raised from the grave of sin and seated with the risen Lord. Sadly, we don't always act as though we have been given this gift of victory.

We are *generous* because we have received God's grace, and we want to follow His example. I remember one year when my dad shared one of his bonuses from work with all four of us children. He didn't have to, but in his gratitude he wanted to. That's how we feel about receiving God's grace—we want to share it with others.

God's grace makes us *courteous*. Because God has not

been critical and angry with us, we avoid being that way with others.

Finally, God's grace makes us *strong*. The beauty of God's strength is that it is made perfect in our weakness. God's strength was shown through the widow's empty pitchers and through David's small sling and can be shown in our weakness when we present ourselves as vessels of His grace.

Because of God's gracious gift to us—His Son—we can share the blessings of victory, generosity, courtesy, and strength in our interactions with our children, our husbands, and our friends. God's grace makes us *rich!*

Father,
The more we get to know You, the more we appreciate Your grace.
Thank You for Your indescribable gift! Amen.

THREE

Grace

Do not be carried away by all kinds of strange teachings. It is good for our hearts to be strengthened by grace, not by ceremonial foods, which are of no value to those who eat them.

HEBREWS 13:9

I have read this verse many times before, but when I read it in my morning devotional time recently, three words jumped out at me—"strengthened by grace." More often I see the words *amazing, abounding,* or *healing* tied together with *grace,* but *strengthened* was a new thought. To strengthen something is to encourage or enlarge it. How does grace encourage and enlarge our hearts?

Grace, like the earth's water system, operates on gravity—the spiritual "gravity of grace." Just as the waters of the Niagara roll over the falls and plunge down to a river below, and just as that river flows ever down to the even lower ranges of its course, then glides to still more low-lying areas where it brings life and growth, so it is with God's grace. Grace's gravity carries it to the lowly in heart, where it brings life and blessing. Grace goes to the humble.

This is the spiritual law behind Proverbs 3:34, which James 4:6 quotes: "God opposes the proud but gives grace to the humble." The unbowed soul standing proudly before God receives no benefit from God's falling grace. It may descend upon him, but it does not penetrate, and drips away like rain from a statue. But the soul lying before God is immersed—and even swims—in a sea of grace. So while there is always more grace, it is reserved for the lowly and the humble. Humility invites the elevating weight of grace.[8]

Strengthening grace comes to the humble—to those who admit their need.

Father,
Thanks that when we admit our neediness to You, You strengthen and enlarge our hearts with Your unending grace. Amen.

Grace

*For the grace of God that brings salvation has appeared to all men.
It teaches us to say "No" to ungodliness and worldly passions,
and to live self-controlled, upright and godly lives in this present age,
while we wait for the blessed hope—the glorious appearing of our
great God and Savior, Jesus Christ, who gave himself for us
to redeem us from all wickedness and to purify for himself
a people that are his very own, eager to do what is good.*

TITUS 2:11-14

Grace brings salvation.

All of God's promises and saving work that He has
shown since the beginning of the human race have revealed
His grace. All of His blessings and all of His gifts have been
planned to bring men and women to repentance. One of the
purposes of Jesus' death on the cross was to redeem us
from iniquity, but that wasn't the only reason. He also
wanted to purify us and encourage us toward good works.

Grace teaches us to say no to ungodliness.

To be godly inwardly is to be self-controlled. Exercising
control of our actions and emotions with our will can only
be accomplished as we depend on God's Spirit to govern

our lives (Galatians 5:22-23). As we experience God's grace, we live honest, faithful, straightforward, and trustworthy lives outwardly among those around us. And finally, godly living displays itself with much more than words—it demonstrates the reality and power of a vital union with God.

Grace causes us to look for the blessed hope.

Knowing that Jesus will return for us is a big incentive to live holy lives now.

What a privilege we experience through God's grace— that of being changed in so many ways!

Father,
Thank You that Your grace brings us salvation, godliness, and hope. May we never forget how much all of that cost You. Amen.

FIVE

Grace

*B*e self-controlled and alert. Your enemy the devil prowls around like a roaring lion looking for someone to devour. Resist him, standing firm in the faith, because you know that your brothers throughout the world are undergoing the same kind of sufferings. And the God of all grace, who called you to his eternal glory in Christ, after you have suffered a little while, will himself restore you and make you strong, firm and steadfast.

1 PETER 5:8-10

Grace does not make everything right. Grace's trick is to show us that it is right for us to live; that it is truly good, wonderful even, for us to be breathing and feeling at the same time that everything clustering around us is wholly wretched. Grace is not a ticket to Fantasy Island; Fantasy Island is dreamy fiction. Grace is not a potion to charm life to our liking; charms are magic. Grace does not cure all our cancers, transform all our kids into winners, or send us all soaring into the high skies of sex and success. Grace is rather an amazing power to look earthy reality full in the face, see its sad and tragic edges, feel its cruel cuts, join in the primeval chorus against its outrageous unfairness, and yet feel in your deepest being that it is good and right for you to be alive on God's good earth.

Grace is power, I say, to see life very clearly, admit it is sometimes all wrong, and still know that somehow, in the center of your life, "It's all right." This is one reason we call it amazing grace. . . . Grace is the one word for all that God is for us in the form of Jesus Christ. — Lewis B. Smedes, *How Can It Be All Right When Everything Is Wrong?*[9]

Any mom who has ever felt despair can appreciate the power of those words. Grace doesn't take away our problem, but God comes alongside us while we are in the midst of it. And He promises to restore us, making us "strong, firm and steadfast."

Father,
Sometimes it does feel like life is all wrong. Thank You that You understand every circumstance of each person reading this, and that You will come to us and meet us with Your grace in our moment of need, if we will just ask. Amen.

EXTRA READINGS FOR DAYS 6 AND 7
Ephesians 2:1-10; Romans 5:15-21

7

Contentment

ONE

Contentment

*I am the good shepherd. The good shepherd
lays down his life for the sheep."*

JOHN 10:11

In order for us to be truly content, we must have an accurate picture of who God is and who we are. Looking at the relationship between a shepherd and his sheep helps us to better understand that picture.

Throughout the Bible God is described as the Good Shepherd, and people are sometimes likened to sheep. King David was a boyhood shepherd himself, and he knew that sheep, like us, are very needy. The lot in life of any one sheep depended on the shepherd who owned it. A shepherd could be kind, thoughtful, and wise, or he could be mean, inconsiderate, and irresponsible. When we see God as our Shepherd, we realize that we have the very best care available. Our Shepherd is all-powerful and all knowing. He never sleeps, and He cares about us individually because He gave us life and sustains us.

In order to be content, a sheep must have freedom from fear, tension, aggravation, and hunger. It is the job of the shepherd to provide these freedoms. God provides us with His Spirit to minister security, peace, hope, and His Word to feed us.

> Contentment should be the hallmark of the man or woman who has put his or her affairs in the hands of God. This especially applies in our affluent age. But the outstanding paradox is the intense fever of discontent among people who are ever speaking of security.[10]

When we as needy people realize that we gain the very presence of God in our lives through the Holy Spirit, we realize the contentment that God intends for each one of us. He *is* the Shepherd of our souls, and only He can provide true contentment.

Father,
Thank You that You describe Yourself as our Shepherd. Thank You that You gave Your life for us. Amen.

TWO

Contentment

Now the serpent was more crafty than any of the wild animals the LORD God had made. He said to the woman, "Did God really say, 'You must not eat from any tree in the garden'?" The woman said to the serpent, "We may eat fruit from the trees in the garden, but God did say, 'You must not eat fruit from the tree that is in the middle of the garden, and you must not touch it, or you will die.'"

GENESIS 3:1-3

How content are we—with our children, with our abilities, with our financial situations? How do we measure contentment anyway? Contentment is the state of being satisfied and not desiring more than what we already have. Ouch! It hurts just to hear those words because I realize that discontent is something I experience too often.

In the newspaper I read about a prominent builder of homes who said that one of his keys to success is always having a fabulously decorated model home to show to his upscale customers. After his customers see the beautiful model homes, he said he wants them to walk away feeling terribly dissatisfied with what they already have.

Those feelings of dissatisfaction come straight from the enemy, similar to what happened between Satan and Eve in the Garden of Eden. When Satan came to Eve, he did not remind her of all the wonderful things God *had* provided for her, but rather he focused on the *one* restriction. This is typical of Satan's behavior—he focuses on the thing we don't have instead of reminding us of all God has given us to enjoy.

God desires for us to come to Him with thanks for all the things that He *has* blessed us with. Giving heed to the if onlys is an awful trap to fall into, and it only causes increased dissatisfaction. When I thank God for all He has blessed me with, I quickly gain a renewed perspective. A grateful person is usually a contented person.

God,
Please forgive us for the times we get a bad case of the if onlys. Thank You for Your many provisions. May we remember them often. Amen.

THREE

Contentment

They all ate and were satisfied, and the disciples picked up twelve basketfuls of broken pieces that were left over.

LUKE 9:17

I like getting up early in the morning, but I wasn't always like this. When I was in high school, I made things hard on my mom because I was stubborn about getting ready for school. Making it to my 8 A.M. classes in college was a huge challenge, and I'm sure I used up all my excused absences.

I must have begun changing my ways after becoming a mother. Getting up very early has often been my only opportunity for quiet time. Quiet time for me includes reading the Bible, praying, and thinking. I don't do any of those things well when the setting is busy or noisy.

This morning I woke up at 6 A.M. in a hotel where my family is staying. We are on a weekend trip to take our son Chad back to college for his junior year. Since we don't have to check out of the hotel until 10 A.M., it was very tempting to stay snuggled under the bedcovers. But I remembered that my attitudes and perspectives for each day are often established in the quiet of the mornings during time spent in God's Word. Once I decided to get up, my next challenge was finding a quiet spot. My family was asleep in the dark room, and the hotel lobby was too noisy. I decided to pull a comfortable chair out into the hall, and here I am with a quiet, cozy spot and a cup of coffee!

My Bible reading this morning reminded me of the power of God, the importance of my faith, and the great contentment that I experience when I am fed spiritually. In the same way that hungry people were satisfied when Jesus fed the 5,000, our souls are *satisfied* when we spend time with God.

God,
The ways that the world seeks contentment are so different from the plan You have for us. Thank You that when we spend time in Your Word, we experience contentment. Amen.

Contentment

Don't let others spoil your faith and joy with their philosophies, their wrong and shallow answers built on men's thoughts and ideas, instead of on what Christ has said. For in Christ there is all of God in a human body; so you have everything when you have Christ, and you are filled with God through your union with Christ. He is the highest Ruler, with authority over every other power.
COLOSSIANS 2:8-10, TLB

To be discontented is to have a restless longing for better circumstances—it's to have a case of the if onlys. If only I had a better job. If only I had more money. If only I had a bigger house. If only my husband was more responsible. The list could go on and on.

The *Chicago Tribune* recently published a weeklong series of articles examining the psychology of contentment. Some suggestions were: get more rest, put on a happy face, get involved in the moment, live fully to your potential, or consider taking mood-altering drugs.

There is no shortage of suggestions from psychologists, therapists, authors and even talk-show hosts about how to improve mood and boost personal happiness levels. One popular theory espouses a predetermined genetic set point of happiness, modifiable only within certain individual limits.[11]

So where *do* we find contentment? In a personal, growing relationship with Christ. Christ meets our needs — whether we are lonely, confused, needing forgiveness, discontented, or full of anxiety. He cares about us and wants us to come to Him with our needs. Only Jesus can satisfy our longing souls.

> *Friends all around us are trying to find*
> *What the heart yearns for, by sin undermined;*
> *I have the secret, I know where 'tis found:*
> *Only in Jesus true pleasures abound.*[12]

May we not attempt to find contentment in shallow things, but may we look to Jesus!

Father,
Thank You that You are more than enough. Thank You that You have authority over every other power. Thanks for the contentment You bring to our souls. Amen.

FIVE

Contentment

I know what it is to be in need, and I know what it is to have plenty.
I have learned the secret of being content in any and every situation,
whether well fed or hungry, whether living in plenty or in want.
I can do everything through him who gives me strength.

PHILIPPIANS 4:12-13

God, grant me the serenity to accept the things I cannot change, courage to change the things I can, and wisdom to know the difference.

The mom who prays this prayer is exercising trust in God because she realizes there are some things in life she can't change. She's not feeling trapped, though, because she's asking for courage to make good choices in things that *can* be changed, and she's admitting that at times it's difficult to identify which is which.

Sometimes a restless discontentment can be an opportunity for change or growth. Perhaps a mom feels she has run up against a brick wall in dealing with her child, or she knows she's having trouble setting limits and boundaries. She can, if necessary, make the choice to seek help from a Christian counselor. But there are some things in life we can't change—like our families of origin, our genes, our children, or our husbands. What do we do with the situations in life that we'd like to change but can't? We all encounter those. We may have no control over the situation, but we can choose the attitude of our hearts.

We learn that our contentment will be directly proportional to our trust in God. If we have little trust, we'll find little contentment. If we have great trust in Him, we will have great contentment. Long-term contentment in our soul is not a matter of situation—it is a matter of trust in God.

Father,
May I always make the choice to trust You. Please give me great wisdom in all the other choices of life. Amen.

EXTRA READINGS FOR DAYS 6 AND 7
John 10:1-18; Genesis 3:1-13

8

Love

ONE

Love

But God demonstrates his own love for us in this: While we were still sinners, Christ died for us.

ROMANS 5:8

Could anything be said more plainly? It is not we who begin negotiations with God to convey to Him our desire for love. It is God who continually presents His love in an assurance beyond argument. He lets the full force of evidence break through our hardened hearts and deaf ears. The logic of God's love shown to us is intended to penetrate our very depths.[13]

Sometimes, for an hour or two or for a day, I am prompted to look for all the ways God seeks to show His love to me. We talk about seeking God, but we sometimes forget about how much He seeks us—constantly. We see His love in the air we breathe, the day and the night, the beauty of the seasons, the magnificent way He created our bodies to function, the plants and animals He created for our food and enjoyment—and the list goes on.

But most of all, His love was revealed when Jesus died for us *"while we were still sinners."* It's the redemptive aspect of His love that ministers health to my soul. He didn't wait until I was "good enough." His loving plan for all of us is to *redeem* us—to save us from a state of sinfulness and restore us with honor, worth, and reputation that are all based on *Him*!

And redemptive love doesn't stop with us. God's plan is for the world, and when we accept His redemption for our souls, we desire to participate in loving others with God's love.

Father,
Thank You that You loved us before we even thought about You! May our gratefulness prompt us to service for You. Amen.

TWO

Love

"My command is this: Love each other as I have loved you."
JOHN 15:12

How do we understand love, and how do we measure it? With five words—"as I have loved you." Jesus left both a standard and a personal example for us to follow. He doesn't ask us to do what He hasn't already done.

First, He laid down His life for us (v . 13). In order for me to love, I may need to *forfeit* something valuable to me for the sake of another person. This may involve giving up some of my desires or expectations or experiencing a greater or lesser degree of inconvenience.

Second, Jesus contrasted slaves and friends to teach us that He not only treats us kindly, but He shares His very thoughts with us (v. 15). He has chosen to *commune* with us and be close to us. This must have been very difficult for Him to do with His disciples when He knew that some would doubt Him, betray Him, deny Him, or run away from Him. Without His grace and strength, it would be impossible for us to carry out His example.

Third, Jesus took initiative and action with his disciples.

He did not sit back and wait for them to come to Him, but He reached out to them (v. 16). How and when we do these things needs to be thought through with integrity and honesty, asking God for His wisdom, strength, and grace, because when we choose to love, the world sees that we are God's disciples.

Father,
Thank You that You love us perfectly. Please forgive us for the lack of love we sometimes have for others. We need the warmth of Your love in hearts that would be cold without You. Amen.

Be imitators of God, therefore, as dearly loved children and live a life of love, just as Christ loved us and gave himself up for us as a fragrant offering and sacrifice to God.

EPHESIANS 5:1-2

Two of my piano students, Corrie and Sydney, are sisters. They look alike, and they talk alike. They are darling; they both have freckles on their cheeks, gentle southern accents, and sweet dispositions. Why? They are imitators of their parents, both in the way they dress and the way they act.

The way we learn to love is by imitating Christ. How did/does He love? When Jesus gave Himself as a sacrifice for sinners—for us—He brought great joy to the heart of God. That's who we should imitate, and that's how we should love—sacrificially. It's not hard to love a person who treats us well or a person we respect. But what about a person who hasn't treated us well or a person we don't respect? Jesus wasn't treated well by mankind—we crucified Him. And how much respect could He have felt toward people who denied Him and abandoned Him? But He still loved mankind so much that He *died* for us!

So what does sacrificial love look like? It involves forfeiting something we value highly for the sake of someone we believe to have a greater value or claim—God and His kingdom. We may choose to forfeit a dream, a comfort, a convenience, or some of our time and money because we want to show God's love to another, bringing great joy to the heart of God! We imitate God through a life of giving and serving.

Father,
Your example would be impossible for us to follow if You hadn't also promised us Your presence and Your strength in our lives. May we look to You daily, wanting to imitate You and receive Your power. Amen.

FOUR

Love

Above all, love each other deeply, because love covers over a multitude of sins.

1 PETER 4:8

Ah, the beauty of being at peace with another, neither having to weigh thoughts or measure words, but spilling them out just as they are; chaff and grain together, certain that a faithful hand will keep what is worth keeping, and with a breath of kindness blow the rest away.

Arab proverb

I'm thankful for friends and family who have seen me at both my better and worse moments but love me just the same. The Christian's love muscle is called on to have amazing elasticity and flexibility. The wife of a company president sits and applauds her husband at a banquet where he is honored for his accomplishments in front of others, and yet she has also known him to do or say things that are less than admirable. We cheer on our child who is given a great honor at his or her school, fully aware of that child's foibles and inconsistencies (as they are of ours!).

Love covers. So where do we draw the line between a

healthy amount of love that covers sins and ignoring sins to the point of enabling a person to go on in destructive behaviors or addictions?

Because of our sinful nature, we all have shortcomings and inconsistencies. As they surface from time to time, we stretch and forgive others as we hope they will do for us. However, if repetitive behaviors become destructive or addictive, God has given us healthy ways of dealing with bigger issues. In these cases, we are not wise to roll over and ignore the problems. (See Matthew 18:15-17, Luke 17:3, or Ephesians 5:3-11.)

Father,
Please give us grace to have flexible love muscles for daily family life, and courage to deal with larger problems that demand special attention. Amen.

*If your brother sins against you, go and show him his fault,
just between the two of you. If he listens to you, you have won
your brother over. But if he will not listen, take one or two others along,
so that every matter may be established by the testimony of two or
three witnesses. If he refuses to listen to them, tell it to the church;
and if he refuses to listen even to the church, treat him
as you would a pagan or a tax collector."*

MATTHEW 18:15-18

It's not difficult to love a person when things in the relationship are going well. But what happens when it feels like someone is our enemy? Sadly, we sometimes meet up with experiences that are very unjust; someone may have stolen from us, or a woman's husband or friend might be involved in immoral behavior. Does God really expect us to love *them?*

God has not left us without provision for these types of situations. To read his Word (the whole of it) is to know that He left us instructions for what to do when another believer has blatantly sinned against us.

First, we go to the person one on one. We don't go with the goal of winning an argument; we go with the goal of speaking the truth in love (Galatians 6:1; Ephesians 4:15).

This meeting may be enough to get things moving on the right track. If so, the relationship is on its way to restoration. If not, there's another step.

Second, we ask for help and counsel from one or two other mature believers, going to the offender *together*. When sin isn't dealt with, it spreads, and so does the circle of people that it influences.

If steps 1 and 2 don't prompt confession and repentance, the third step is to take the matter to the church. By this time, if the offender has not repented, he or she forfeits his or her position of spiritual brother or sister and is not held in close fellowship.

The goal of these loving but tough steps is restoration of the person and the relationship, and for this we hope and pray.

Father,
We realize that life's situations are sometimes extremely challenging, and we're thankful that You have not left us without help from Your Word. Please give us extra strength and wisdom to meet the challenges that come our way. Amen.

EXTRA READINGS FOR DAYS 6 AND 7
1 Corinthians 13; John 15:1-17

9

Forgiveness

ONE

Forgiveness

If my people, who are called by my name, will humble themselves and pray and seek my face and turn from their wicked ways, then will I hear from heaven and forgive their sins and heal their land."

2 CHRONICLES 7:14

When something isn't quite right with my child's knee, causing pain, irritation, and limited motion, it's helpful when the doctor says measures can be taken to help the knee function well again. It's like that with our hearts too. Our hearts are often in need of mending, and God has left us with steps that we can take to promote healing and wholeness for the innermost parts of our souls.

The first thing God asks us to do is *humble ourselves.* When we take this posture before God, we remind ourselves that He is God and we are not! We come to Him as needy human beings, admitting that we fall short of His righteous standards.

The second step we take is to *pray.* We call out to God for help that only He can give. Whether we are asking forgiveness for our own heart or asking for help in showing forgiveness to another, God's grace only comes from Him—it doesn't come from within ourselves.

God also asks us to *seek His face*. Seeking God is more than having a casual interest in Him. It's similar to going on a hunt, and the place for us to start is God's Word, where He reveals Himself to us.

Serious seeking prompts us to *turn from things that don't please God*, because His Spirit comes alongside us and shows us areas of our lives where we need to do some about-faces. As we take these steps God has given us, He is faithful to forgive us and heal us.

Father,
May we experience healing through humbling ourselves, praying, seeking Your face, and turning from sin. Amen.

TWO

Forgiveness

Blessed is he whose transgressions are forgiven, whose sins are covered.
Blessed is the man whose sin the LORD does not count against him
and in whose spirit is no deceit.

PSALM 32:1-2

The Bible contains over 100 direct references to forgiveness, pointing out that sin needs to be removed before relationships can be restored, both our relationships with God and relationships with others. Here's an overview:

1. We humans have a driving need in our hearts for forgiveness.

2. According to Psalm 32, when we are in need of forgiveness, we waste and groan, carrying around a sense of heaviness in our spirit that saps our strength.

3. God does not play games with us. Rather, when we decide to come to Him for forgiveness, He decisively discards our sin, because His Son's blood already paid our penalty on the cross.

4. Not only does He remove our sin—He says He removes it "as far as the east is from the west" (Psalm 103:12)—that is, immeasurably, infinitely.

5. When we quit covering up our sin, our groaning and sighing are replaced with singing. Even if there's not actual music, our hearts are glad and happiness returns.

6. God's mercy is very wide. Psalm 103:13 teaches us that God pities us the way a father pities his children.

7. Instead of fearing God and avoiding Him, we find Him to be our hiding place. He becomes the one we run to for protection.

The person who is forgiven is *blessed!*

Father,
Not what these hands have done can save this guilty soul; / Not what this toiling flesh has borne can make my spirit whole. / Thy work alone, O Christ, can ease this weight of sin; / Thy blood alone, O Lamb of God, can give me peace within.[14]

THREE
Forgiveness

"This is how my heavenly Father will treat each of you unless you forgive your brother from your heart."
MATTHEW 18:35

A man had been stealing money from the king, and when the injustice was discovered, the man had stolen 10,000 talents—probably the equivalent of 10 million dollars in today's terms. In addition to having stolen money, this was one proud man. He seemed more upset about getting caught than about having stolen. He actually thought that, given enough time, he could pay the king back. This man would have been in very deep weeds if the king hadn't been a man of compassion. He took the loss on himself and forgave the servant. As a result of the king's mercy, the man was not thrown into debtor's prison.

When the forgiven man left the king, he found a fellow servant who owed him a very small sum of money. Grabbing and choking the servant, he demanded payment; and when the debtor fell to his knees asking for patience, the man ordered the debtor thrown into prison until he could pay up.

When the king heard what had happened, he ordered the wicked servant thrown into jail to be tormented. He dealt with him the way the wicked servant had dealt with his debtor.

Jesus warned us that God cannot forgive us if we do not have humble and repentant hearts. We reveal the true condition of our hearts by the way we treat others. When our hearts are humble and repentant, we will gladly forgive our brothers. But where there is pride and a desire for revenge, there can be no true repentance.[15]

Father,
What a graphic picture You give us in Your Word of what pride does to us. May we humble ourselves before You, so that we might find grace for ourselves and then be willing to share it with another. Amen.

Forgiveness

When they sin against you—for there is no one who does not sin—and you become angry with them and give them over to the enemy, who takes them captive to his own land, far away or near; and if they have a change of heart in the land where they are held captive, and repent and plead with you in the land of their conquerors and say, 'We have sinned, we have done wrong, we have acted wickedly'; and if they turn back to you with all their heart and soul in the land of their enemies who took them captive, and pray to you toward the land you gave their fathers, toward the city you have chosen and the temple I have built for your Name; then from heaven, your dwelling place, hear their prayer and their plea, and uphold their cause. And forgive your people, who have sinned against you; forgive all the offenses they have committed against you, and cause their conquerors to show them mercy."

1 KINGS 8:46-50

Building a temple for the glory of God was a huge task for a young king. At its dedication, Solomon prayed for the people's hearts, more important than the new temple.

Solomon didn't say "if" in regard to sin, because he knew it was a matter of "when." His wise words gave the people a pattern for what they should do when they sinned, and it's still a pattern for believers today:

1. We *will* sin.
2. *When* we sin, *if* we have a change of heart, and repent and plead to God, *if* we turn back to God with all our heart and soul, and pray to God, *then*:
3. God will hear our prayer, forgive the offenses we have committed against Him, and show us mercy.

This is a pattern for us to use and teach to our children. University of Chicago divinity professor Jean Bethke Elshtain said:

> "Contrition chic" is becoming part of America's political culture, but often many of the elements of true contrition are missing.[16]

We must follow God's pattern for repentance and forgiveness. How gracious that God does not leave us to carry our own burden of sin—He carried it to the cross. And when we follow the pattern He gave us for repentance, we become channels of His mercy.

Merciful God,
Thank You that we do not have to carry our sin, but that You show us mercy when we turn to You with all our heart and soul. Amen.

FIVE

Forgiveness

"Forgive us our debts, as we also have forgiven our debtors.'"
MATTHEW 6:12

One day Jeanne S. Zechmeister, a psychologist at Loyola University, observed a woman at Mass who recited the Lord's Prayer with the rest of the congregants but, very deliberately, did not say the lines about forgiveness.

"The only thing that Jesus asks of us in the Lord's Prayer is that we forgive others; the rest of the prayer is petition," Zechmeister said. "I keep wondering why the woman would not say it. I'd like to talk to her."[17]

To forgive a person is to stop blaming him or her for a wrong, to bury the hatchet and, in releasing our desire for revenge, be released from anger. How does this take place? That's the million-dollar question!

Lewis Smedes, author of *The Art of Forgiving*, has some helpful guidelines on forgiving:

—Forgiving happens in three stages: We rediscover the humanity of the person who wronged us, we surrender our right to get even, and we wish that person well.

—We forgive people only for what they do, never for what they are.

—We cannot forgive a wrong unless we first blame the person who wronged us.

—Forgiving is a journey; the deeper the wound, the longer the journey.

—Forgiving is not a way to avoid pain but to heal pain.

—Forgivers are not doormats; to forgive a person is not a signal that we are willing to put up with what he does.

—When we forgive, we walk in stride with the forgiving God.[18]

Forgiving is hard work, but we are probably never more like God than when we forgive.

Father,

Learning to forgive is not easy. When we decide that we really want to forgive another person, please give us Your wisdom and the strength to obey Your command. Amen.

EXTRA READINGS FOR DAYS 6 AND 7
Psalm 32; Matthew 18:21-35

10

Peace

ONE

Peace

I will lie down and sleep in peace, for you alone, O LORD, make me dwell in safety.

PSALM 4:8

During my early thirties, my husband traveled a fair amount for his job. I was not accustomed to being alone at night and found that I wasn't sleeping very well. When I mentioned my situation to a friend, she related an experience I'll never forget. Theo and her husband were missionaries to West Africa—Americans living in a foreign culture. Security was enough of an issue even when her husband was around, but when he traveled on occasion, she felt apprehensive at night. While her husband was away on a trip, she awoke one morning to discover that she had left a door to the courtyard not only unlocked but *open* the night before. After checking through the house and realizing that everything was all right, she reasoned that if God could take care of her and keep her safe when the door was open overnight, then she need not worry about being home alone! From then on when her husband was gone at night, she remembered Psalm 4:8.

In Mark 4 Jesus and his disciples were in a boat on the Sea of Galilee when a fierce storm came up suddenly. In the middle of the storm, Jesus was able to take a nap. Why? Because He knew He was secure in God's will, and He knew that God would care for Him. That's peace!

Are you experiencing storms in your life? Are you in turmoil? Remember that God wants us to come to Him for our peace and security. *He* is our peace! *He* is our security!

Father,
Instead of worrying and being fearful, may we run to You when we feel insecure, realizing that You want to give us Your peace. Amen.

TWO

Peace

"Peace I leave with you; my peace I give you. I do not give to you as the world gives. Do not let your hearts be troubled and do not be afraid."
JOHN 14:27

At the moment when Jesus imparted peace to His disciples, peace—in the world's sense—seemed the farthest from Him. His crucifixion was imminent, and yet He was sharing His peace with those around Him. The kind of peace Jesus gives is not freedom from suffering, but a calm, constant devotion to the will of God.

H. G. Spafford was a businessman in Chicago. He was a dedicated Christian. He had some serious financial reversals, and during the time of readjustment, he lost his home. Realizing his family needed to get away for a vacation, Spafford decided to take the entire family to England. He sent his wife and four daughters ahead on the *S.S. Ville du Havre*. In mid-ocean the French steamer carrying his loved ones collided with another and sank within twelve minutes; 230 people lost their lives. The four daughters were drowned, but Mrs. Spafford was rescued. She wired her husband, "Saved alone." Mr. Spafford was almost overcome with grief. He had lost his property, his four precious daughters were buried beneath the dark waves of the sea, and his wife was prostrate with grief on the other side of the world. But he put all his trust in God and wrote a song that has comforted thousands since that time:

> *When peace, like a river attendeth my way;*
> *When sorrows like sea-billows roll —*
> *Whatever my lot, Thou hast taught me to say,*
> *It is well, it is well with my soul.*[19]

Father,
Thank You that You share Your peace with us in a much different way than we expect. It's always available — even in the worst of times. May we be devoted to You consistently so that we will experience Your peace consistently. Amen.

THREE
Peace

*D*o not be anxious about anything, but in everything, by prayer and
petition, with thanksgiving, present your requests to God.
And the peace of God, which transcends all understanding,
will guard your hearts and your minds in Christ Jesus.

PHILIPPIANS 4:6-7

Worry is a thin stream of fear trickling through the mind.
If encouraged, it cuts a channel into which all other
thoughts are drained.

Arthur Somers Rocke

The stream of worry is built one drop or one thought at
a time. Worry is made up of many, many anxious thoughts.
It's not enough to say to ourselves, "Self, stop worrying!"
Left on our own, we'll come back to it. Rather, God gives us
something specific to do when we feel anxious or worried.
He tells us to present our requests to Him about *everything*,
and we are to give them over to God in three ways:

1. Prayer—talking to God about the situation.
2. Petition—a request we make to an authority.
3. Thanksgiving—an expression of gratitude.

When we present something to someone, there's often some ceremony involved. We need to literally hand over our worries and get rid of them. We do this by coming to God, calling on His authority as God, thanking Him for the things He's already done, and expressing our confidence in Him for the future. As we make that presentation, an exchange takes place. We hand over our worry, and God's peace comes to guard our hearts. The word "guard" is used here as a military term, so we might picture a sentinel watching over our hearts and minds.

As always with God, He gives us the better end of the deal. We give Him our worries, our requests, and our thanks, and He gives us His peace.

God, my authority,

I confess my worry, and I hand it over to You. Thank You that You are in control and that You hear me. Please give me Your peace to stand guard over my heart and mind. Thanks for all You've done for me in the past and all that You'll do in the future. Amen.

Peace

A heart at peace gives life to the body, but envy rots the bones.
PROVERBS 14:30

This verse displays a contrast that gets our attention—the difference between life and decay, stemming from peace or envy. All throughout the Bible, peace is described as hope, trust, and quiet in the soul that is brought about by reconciliation with God, through faith in Christ. Quite the opposite, however, is the picture of envy. To be an envious person is to be discontented, dealing with resentment and yearning.

I recently came across a newspaper article detailing some of the scientific studies suggesting that religious faith benefits health. These studies don't go to God's Word as their authority, but they rely on surveys that are demonstrating to the world the truth of what the believer already knows. Our personal faith in God through Christ helps us grow in peace. The further we progress in our faith, the more settled we become. This isn't to say that we don't ever become sick, encounter serious problems, or have anxious thoughts, but we have an anchor for our souls. When our little ship feels as though it's being tossed about and we're not sure where we are, it's comforting to know that whatever happens to us here, we'll someday be safe in heaven's harbor with God forever. *That's* peace.

Is your little ship tossing about? Do things feel out of control? Do you lack a compass amidst storms in your life? Jesus came to seek and save people who were otherwise lost. Run to Him. Run to His Word. To be in relationship with Him is to experience peace!

Father,
Thank You that we can experience peace through a relationship with You. May we choose to pursue it! Amen.

FIVE

Peace

I have told you these things, so that in me you may have peace.
In this world you will have trouble. But take heart!
I have overcome the world."
JOHN 16:33

Many people think of peace as being the absence of war or conflict, but Jesus taught a different kind of peace. He never taught that peace would be found or experienced when there was no conflict or war, because as Christians we live in a constant war zone. Our enemy, the devil, seeks to destroy us and undermine our faith, and as long as we are alive, we are not in a parade—we are in a battle.

The peace that Jesus offers us is found *in Him*, as opposed to the tribulation that is found *in the world*. Romans 5:1 tells us, "Therefore, since we have been justified through faith, we have *peace* with God through our Lord Jesus Christ." The peace that Jesus brings is a combination of hope, trust, and quiet in our minds and souls, which can be realized and experienced even when life experiences are *not* peaceful.

Peace, perfect peace—in this dark world of sin?
The blood of Jesus whispers peace within.
Peace, perfect peace—by thronging duties pressed?
To do the will of Jesus, this is rest.
Peace, perfect peace—with sorrows surging round?
On Jesus' bosom naught but calm is found.
Peace, perfect peace—our future all unknown?
Jesus we know, and He is on the throne.
Peace, perfect peace—death shadowing us and ours?
Jesus has vanquished death and all its powers.
It is enough; earth's struggles soon shall cease;
And Jesus call us to heaven's perfect peace.[20]

Father,
Thank You for the hope, trust, and quiet that only You can bring to our
hearts and minds as we trust You. Amen.

EXTRA READINGS FOR DAYS 6 AND 7
Psalm 4; Philippians 4:1-13

11

Perseverance

ONE

Perseverance

Then Jesus told his disciples a parable to show them that they should always pray and not give up. He said: "In a certain town there was a judge who neither feared God nor cared about men. And there was a widow in that town who kept coming to him with the plea, 'Grant me justice against my adversary.' For some time he refused. But finally he said to himself, 'Even though I don't fear God or care about men, yet because this widow keeps bothering me, I will see that she gets justice, so that she won't eventually wear me out with her coming.'"

LUKE 18:1-5

Although the judge in this parable had no interest in the Jewish widow's situation, the widow *kept coming* to the courtroom of the judge. She was not asking for punishment or revenge on her adversary—she was looking for justice. If it hadn't been for the persistence of the woman, the judge might not have been persuaded to do anything. But because her visits were tiresome and annoying, the judge decided to deal with the matter.

We are meant to see a huge contrast between the unjust judge in this parable and a just and merciful God. If out of the purely selfish motive of being rid of an annoying woman an ungodly judge would grant a defenseless woman her request, how much more will a God who is full of truth and grace hear and answer the prayers of His children whom He loves.

The emphasis in this parable is not meant to encourage us to weary God with our requests (we can't), but rather to assure us that He is very willing to take care of His children. Someone has said, "The purpose of prayer is not to get man's will done in heaven, but to get God's will done on earth." It is good for us to be persistent, as long as we want God's will and aren't selfishly demanding our own agenda.

God,
Thank You for parables in the New Testament that help us to understand how much You love us. Because we know You do, may we come to You often with our needs and requests, persevering in faith and prayer. Amen.

TWO

Perseverance

*By faith he [Moses] left Egypt, not fearing the king's anger;
he persevered because he saw him who is invisible.*

HEBREWS 11:27

We often think of perseverance as straining and gritting our teeth to get a job done. We're correct in realizing that a person who perseveres is not a person who quits and that diligence and persistence are necessary for achieving our goals and living out our beliefs. But too often we act as though all the strength to persevere must come from *us*. Remembering that *we* are not our only resource for perseverance is wonderfully encouraging.

> One day a little boy was trying to turn over a big rock as his father watched, bemused. The little fellow was grunting and straining and heaving, but he couldn't turn the rock over. His dad asked with a whimsical smile on his face, "Son, are you using all of your strength?" "Yes, Daddy, I'm using all my strength." "No, you're not. You haven't asked me to help you. I'm your father, and my strength is your strength."[21]

The more we see how small we are and how big God is, the more we run to Him, and that's when we see His great power to help us. Moses remembered the God who spoke to him in the burning bush. He remembered the God who changed a rod into a serpent. And when the time came for Moses to do the very hard task of leaving Egypt and leading his people, "he persevered because he saw him who is invisible."

Father,
Thank You for Your great strength. May we continue to persevere because we are looking to You. Amen.

THREE

Perseverance

So, if you think you are standing firm, be careful that you don't fall!
No temptation has seized you except what is common to man.
And God is faithful; he will not let you be tempted beyond what you
can bear. But when you are tempted, he will also provide a way out
so that you can stand up under it.

1 CORINTHIANS 10:12-13

It's encouraging for us to realize that encountering temptation is not a sin, because even Jesus was tempted (Hebrews 4:15). But our pattern of response to temptation indicates our spiritual state.

When we deal with temptations of the body, God has already provided us with a way of escape. Adrian Rogers calls it "the King's highway—two legs and a hard run." When Joseph realized that Potiphar's wife was trying to seduce him, he fled. First Corinthians 6:18 tells us, "Flee from sexual immorality." We're not told to fight—we're told to flee!

We are taught to deal with temptations in our souls by loving God.

> *Turn your eyes upon Jesus,*
> *Look full in His wonderful face,*
> *And the things of earth will grow strangely dim,*
> *In the light of His glory and grace.*[22]

If we're experiencing God in our lives, we won't quickly run to substitutes.

When Jesus knew that the devil was trying to get between Him and God, Jesus told the devil, "Out of my sight, Satan! You are a stumbling block to me; you do not have in mind the things of God, but the things of men" (Matthew 16:23). We can do the same, in the name of Jesus Christ.

We do not want to be like "an ox going to the slaughter, like a deer stepping into a noose . . . a bird darting into a snare" (Proverbs 7:21-23). Instead, we can flee, focus on God, and pray!

God our Savior,
Thank You that because You lived on this earth as a man, we know that You understand temptation. Thank You that You left us a pattern and that we have the presence of Your Spirit. May we walk closely with You so that we will find strength to make good choices. Amen.

Perseverance

As you know, we consider blessed those who have persevered.
JAMES 5:11A

Has your husband recently lost a job? Do you have a child who is going through great emotional or physical turmoil? Are you experiencing financial difficulties? Do you feel like throwing in the towel? Pastor and author Kent Hughes suggests that our character and moral development are largely dependent on the experience of suffering. Let's look at what he has to say about persevering in trouble:

> For one thing, trouble promotes trust. We children of God seldom trust God as we do when we are in big trouble. Troubles knock secondary things away. They sharpen our focus and increase our grip on God. When all our attempts at self-deliverance fail, we are forced to trust in the only One who can truly help us. Troubles bring us near to God. When our regular comforts do not suffice, we draw near to Him. It is hard to learn to swim on dry land, but when we are in the water we have to swim. Our troubles are waters in which we are obliged to swim toward God. Troubles strengthen our communication with God. Without troubles we would not learn prayer.

James says in effect, "we consider blessed those who have persevered" because they learn trust, because they draw near to God, and because their communion with God becomes what it ought to be. These are great blessings. Jesus said, "Blessed are those who are persecuted because of righteousness, for theirs is the kingdom of heaven. . . . Rejoice and be glad, because great is your reward in heaven" (Matthew 5:10, 12a). Those who persevere are blessed.[23]

God,
Where can we run when there seems to be trouble all around us? To You! Please help us to trust You more, draw near to You, and commune with You, so that we can keep going and not throw in the towel. Amen.

FIVE

Perseverance

You have heard of Job's perseverance and have seen what the Lord finally brought about. The Lord is full of compassion and mercy.
JAMES 5:11B

Can you imagine having ten children, and then losing *all* of them the same day? Job did.

Job was a prosperous man in every way. He was healthy and wealthy—a man who feared God. Satan thought that Job would remain faithful to God only if he prospered financially, and God permitted Job to be tested. Hardship after hardship came to him; he lost his children, his cattle, his servants, and he was left penniless. "In all this Job did not sin nor charge God with wrong" (Job 1:22).

Although it's hard to imagine things getting any worse, they did. God allowed Job to be afflicted with painful sores from head to toe, but even when Job's wife suggested that he give up his faith, Job said, "Shall we indeed accept good from God, and shall we not accept adversity?" (Job 2:10). Satan's argument in Job's life (and in all our lives) was that "no one serves God for who he is, but for what he or she can get."[24]

But when everything was taken away from Job, he said, "Naked came I from my mother's womb, and naked will I depart. The LORD gave and the LORD has taken away; may the name of the LORD be praised" (Job 1:20-21).

In the end, God blessed Job with spiritual humility and abundant physical blessings, but in the middle of suffering, Job persevered with faith even when he didn't understand the reasoning behind his suffering.

Father,
You know how weak we are. Even when we persevere, we have our moments of tears and questions. Job did too. Please help us to understand that the trials and hardships we experience now are part of a much bigger plan that we don't always understand. May we see Your grace and compassion even in the midst of hard times. Amen.

EXTRA READINGS FOR DAYS 6 AND 7
Psalm 37; James 5:7-12

12

Salvation

ONE

Salvation

For the grace of God that brings salvation has appeared to all men.
TITUS 2:11

During the summers my youngest son and I go to our community's swimming pool every day that the weather allows. I'm always impressed with the many lifeguards stationed every few feet around the pool. Usually they are a quiet presence, but one day my son saw a lifeguard perform the service she was trained to do—deliver a swimmer from difficulty and drowning.

A little girl around the age of five had jumped off the highest diving board. After entering the water, she came up for air but was unable to swim from the middle of the pool over to the edge. The lifeguard blew her whistle, promptly jumped in, and rescued the little girl, who was upset but all right once she got out of the water.

My son has heard the word *salvation* many times, but now he has a mental picture of it—deliverance from difficulty or death. Just as every swimmer in the pool is within sight of a lifeguard, so every person in the world is within the sight of God. Salvation through Jesus has appeared to *all*, and all of us need to realize that we cannot make it through life on our own. The Bible teaches us that in order for us to experience salvation, we need to believe that Jesus is God and turn to Him in saving faith.

Through a common experience of going to the pool, we witnessed a not-so-common rescue, but it was a reminder to me and to my son that God's plan for the whole world is salvation.

God,
We're thankful whenever a person is rescued from difficulty or distress.
Thank You that because of Your death on the cross, we can be rescued
from our sin. Amen.

TWO

Salvation

*They trust in their wealth and boast about how rich they are, yet not one
of them, though rich as kings, can ransom his own brother from the
penalty of sin! For God's forgiveness does not come that way.
For a soul is far too precious to be ransomed by mere earthly wealth.
There is not enough of it in all the earth to buy eternal life for just one
soul, to keep it out of hell. Rich man! Proud man! Wise man!
You must die like all the rest! You have no greater lease on life
than foolish, stupid men. You must leave your wealth to others.*
PSALM 49:6-10, TLB

When I drove several hours to my son's state band
competition today, I was thankful for expressways that
have divided traffic. Many accidents have probably been
avoided because of separation from oncoming cars. I
realize that we spend our lives trying to avoid many things;
we design airbags to help prevent serious injuries in car
crashes, and we invent anesthesia to avoid pain. But none
of our efforts can ever help us avoid eventual death. We can
postpone it perhaps, but never avoid it.

We can't purchase an escape from death with either
time or money, and we can't purchase eternal life either.

Each person that lives on this earth has a penalty to pay for sin, but it can't be worked off with good deeds or paid off with money. God's Word tells us that human souls are far too precious to be ransomed by earthly wealth.

So, if time or money can't rescue us, what can? *Christ's blood through faith!* Romans 3:25 (TLB) teaches, "For God sent Christ Jesus to take the punishment for our sins and to end all God's anger against us. He used Christ's blood and our faith as the means of saving us from his wrath." It's great to design airbags and invent pain-killers, which improve the quality of our short years on earth. But comparatively speaking, we would do well to spend more time thinking about ways to improve the quality of people's *forever* lives — time spent with Jesus that doesn't end!

Father,
Thank You for the priceless provision of Christ's blood that gives us eternal life if we trust in You. Thank You that You place such a great value on our souls. Amen.

THREE

Salvation

John said to the crowds coming out to be baptized by him, "You brood of vipers! Who warned you to flee from the coming wrath? Produce fruit in keeping with repentance. And do not begin to say to yourselves, 'We have Abraham as our father.' For I tell you that out of these stones God can raise up children for Abraham."

LUKE 3:7-8

In John the Baptist's task of preparing the way for Jesus, he went straight to root issues—he called people to repentance. He taught that there will be a future judgment and warned that the only way to avoid God's wrath is to turn from sin and trust God. To repent is to have a change of mind or attitude that includes a reversal of previous thinking or conduct. John told the people that God wasn't impressed with their religious profession if their lives didn't produce fruit. He realized that he had to tell them there would be a judgment before they could receive God's grace.

John's job was to "make straight in the wilderness a highway for our God" (Isaiah 40:3). In ancient times, roads were built whenever a king traveled. His subjects built highways so his chariot would not get stuck in the mud or sand. Just as those subjects prepared roads for their king, John was preparing the way for Jesus by preaching that all people needed salvation.

Just as John reminded the people of his day that salvation wasn't inherited as a result of being descendants of Abraham, it's important for us to teach our children that their salvation is not inherited from us. Rather, it is a result of *their* repentance—a change in mind or attitude going the opposite direction from sin and destruction. And when the posture of their heart leans toward repentance, their lives will show evidence of changed minds and attitudes.

Father,
Thank You that repentance produces fruit in our lives. May we point our children toward You, so they will experience personal repentance and forgiveness in a relationship with You and will produce fruit for Your kingdom. Amen.

FOUR

Salvation

"The Spirit of the Lord is on me, because he has anointed me to preach good news to the poor. He has sent me to proclaim freedom for the prisoners and recovery of sight for the blind, to release the oppressed, to proclaim the year of the Lord's favor."

LUKE 4:18-19

When Jesus taught in his hometown, he chose to read the above verses from Isaiah's prophecy, demonstrating salvation's balance between grace and truth. Since we moms desire to point our children to Christ, it's good for us to think about the balance ourselves.

1. The truth is that we're all poor, but the grace is that God has given us *His* riches.

2. The truth is that on our own we're all prisoners to sin, but the grace is that there is freedom in Christ.

3. The truth is that left to ourselves we are spiritually blind, but the grace is that God can give us sight.

4. The truth is that we are oppressed, but the grace is that by faith in Jesus' death for us, we can be released from oppression.

Imagine a poor orphan child discovering that his parents had left a special bank account for all his needs. Imagine a child locked up in a room but then being freed by the one person who had the key. Imagine a child being chased by a bully until the police officer arrested the bully. We are all that child!

The truth is that we're very needy, but the grace is that Jesus loved us so much that He provided for our needs when He died on the cross. God's salvation makes us very rich.

Father,
Thank You for the best gift in the world—the gift of salvation through Jesus' blood. Thank You that as a result of our faith in You, You bless us with spiritual riches, freedom, sight, and release from oppression. Amen.

FIVE

Salvation

"The Sunrise from on high" is one of the ways the birth of Jesus is described. Four hundred years had passed with no sign of the Savior who had been prophesied. But the dawn was about to break. Some of the characters taking part in this Sunrise to beat all sunrises were Gabriel, Zechariah and Elizabeth, Joseph and Mary, the shepherds, and Simeon. The angel Gabriel appeared to Zechariah and announced the birth of John, who would prepare the way for the Lord.

Mary was also visited by Gabriel and was told that she would give birth to God's Son. The shepherds were the first to hear the good news of Jesus' birth, seeing the light of God's glory shine on their flocks. It was no coincidence that righteous Simeon arrived at the temple exactly when Joseph and Mary took Jesus there to present him to God, because God had promised Simeon that he would not die until he had seen Christ. In a very tender moment Simeon took the child in his arms and said that he was ready to die since God's promise to him had been fulfilled and he had seen Jesus, the Light. And so dawned the Sunrise that brought light and peace to all who will accept it. Like Simeon, we must look for, have faith in, and accept Jesus, the Sunrise on high for *our* souls.

God,
Thank You that Your birth was like the dawn of sunrise, fulfilling the prophecy that You came to provide forgiveness for our sins. Amen.

EXTRA READINGS FOR DAYS 6 AND 7
John 3:1-21; Titus 2:11-14

13

Heaven

ONE

Heaven

There are many homes up there where my Father lives, and I am going to prepare them for your coming."
JOHN 14:2, TLB

After Grandma died, my sister and her husband had several opportunities to talk with their three-year-old son about death. They explained to Brent that Great-Grandma was in heaven with God and that she was very happy there. A few days later we all went to her memorial service, which was held at a local funeral home. As we left, young Brent remarked, "I didn't think heaven would look like *that!*"

What do we expect heaven to look like? It's challenging for moms to know exactly how to respond when our children ask us about heaven because we haven't been there yet. But here are some things we know and can share with our children:

1. Heaven is where God is (Matthew 6:9).

2. Kids love treasure chests, and heaven will be one big treasure chest. For those of us who have loved and served God with our hearts, heaven will include gift after gift after gift (Matthew 6:19-21).

3. Jesus has gone there ahead of us to make it ready and to prepare a place for us (John 14:2).

4. God is surrounded in heaven by angels who serve him. Heaven will be an experience of praising God with the angels forever (Revelation 4).

5. Heaven will feel like home to us—the place where we belong (Philippians 3:20).

6. Heaven will be a safe and happy place where there will be no end to joy! There will be no tears, no pain, no death, no weakness, no night, and no need for sleep (Revelation 21:3-4).

God of heaven,
May I take advantage of opportunities to teach my children some of the things Your Word has told us about heaven. Thank You that heaven will be a place of great joy! Amen.

TWO

Heaven

But each one should be careful how he builds. For no one can lay any foundation other than the one already laid, which is Jesus Christ. If any man builds on this foundation using gold, silver, costly stones, wood, hay or straw, his work will be shown for what it is, because the Day will bring it to light.

1 CORINTHIANS 3:10-15

If you could build your dream house, what would it look like? Would it be a small cottage by the ocean, a condominium in a high-rise close to cultural events in the city, or a brick mansion out in the country with a large circular drive? How big would it be, what period of architecture would you choose, and what kind of building materials would you use?

Few people have the opportunity to live in their dream home. Most people are thankful for adequate shelter that meets their needs and houses the family comfortably. If there are extra comforts and beauties, that's great too! Something that we probably don't spend enough time thinking about is what our home in heaven will be like. God's Word tells us that the way we live our lives here on earth will have an eternal effect on our dwelling in heaven.

If we want our eternal lives to be spent with Jesus, our foundation must be built on Him. Having established that, our daily choices determine the kind of building materials we will use—straw, hay, wood (cheap and easy), or stone, silver, or gold (costly and valuable).

We might imagine that some of us are sending ahead sufficient materials for pup tents, some for studio apartments, some for trailer homes, some for ranch houses, and others for great mansions.[25]

Perhaps a dream home for eternity is something worth thinking about. We are determining what it will be like by the choices we make today.

God my foundation,
It's sobering to remember that my daily choices now will have eternal consequences. May my daily choices of thought, word, and deed be valuable like gold and not cheap like straw. Amen.

THREE
Heaven

We know that the whole creation has been groaning as in the pains of childbirth right up to the present time. Not only so, but we ourselves, who have the firstfruits of the Spirit, groan inwardly as we wait eagerly for our adoption as sons, the redemption of our bodies.

ROMANS 8:22

There have been times when I think we do not desire heaven, but more often I find myself wondering whether in our heart of hearts, we have ever desired anything else.

C. S. Lewis

When we begin a relationship with God through Jesus Christ, we begin a journey to a heavenly kingdom. Seeds of God's righteousness are planted in our souls, and we have new longings for wonder—for things that are wholesome, pure, true, and lovely. We groan to be released from the bondage this world has to sin—the pain, decay, and death that we see as present realities.

Think of the contrast between:

1. A gorgeous summer day spent with friends at the beach / a tornado leaving death and destruction.

2. An especially tender and meaningful connection with a spouse / an ugly disagreement that leaves two people feeling alienated.

3. A hot apple pie fresh from the oven / a container of moldy food in the refrigerator.

I like the sound of the first half of all the above, but not the second half. I like things to be *right!* The reality of life here on earth is that although we experience the pain of living in a fallen world, we get glimpses and tastes of heaven when we look to God. May we be quick to see the promises of heaven in a beautiful sunset, a treasured friendship, or an unexpected gift that only God could have arranged!

Eternal God,
May the painful realities of life not lead me to bitterness or despair but rather toward hope in my eternal future with You. Thank You for moments of wonder and beauty that give little tastes of heaven. Amen.

FOUR

Heaven

*Lord, help me to realize how brief my time on earth will be.
Help me to know that I am here for but a moment more.
My life is no longer than my hand! My whole lifetime is but
a moment to you. Proud man! Frail as breath! A shadow!
And all his busy rushing ends in nothing. He heaps up riches
for someone else to spend. And so, Lord, my only hope is in you.*
PSALM 39:4-7, TLB

Alfred Nobel was a Swedish chemist who made his
fortune by inventing dynamite and other powerful
explosives, which were bought by governments to
produce weapons. When Nobel's brother died, one
newspaper accidentally printed Alfred's obituary instead.
He was described as a man who became rich from
enabling people to kill each other in unprecedented
quantities. Shaken from this assessment, Nobel resolved
to use his fortune to reward accomplishments that
benefited humanity, including what we now know as the
Nobel Peace Prize. Nobel had a rare opportunity—to
look at the assessment of his life at its end, but to still be
alive and have opportunity to change that assessment.[26]

Isn't it interesting how close calls can jar us, wake us up, or get us thinking about what's really important in life? Maybe it was the serious accident of a child that reminded us that relationships are so much more important than schedules. Maybe being confronted by a friend helped us see that our life was out of balance. Maybe reading Psalm 39:4-7 reminded us that in the end, the thing that matters most is our hope in God and how we've been able to influence our children to place their hope in God.

As we assess our lives at the present, what choices can we make today that affirm our hope in the Lord?

God,
Today I want to pray the verses above back to You. Amen.

FIVE

Heaven

*o not store up for yourselves treasures on earth, where moth and rust
destroy, and where thieves break in and steal. But store up for
yourselves treasures in heaven, where moth and rust do not destroy,
and where thieves do not break in and steal.
For where your treasure is, there your heart will be also."*
MATTHEW 6:19-21

We sometimes hear people say, jokingly, "The only things
certain about life are death and taxes." The only thing certain
about riches is that they pass away and don't satisfy. Moths
and rust are both pictures moms can identify with, pictures
that remind us of the perishable nature of earthly goods. We
use mothballs to prevent female moths from leaving our
garments full of holes. The damage these little critters cause
happens slowly and quietly, like rust on our cars.

What are *our* treasures? What has great value to us? Is
it money, clothes, our house? All the treasures in the world
are not enough to satisfy our souls.

Money solved *some* of the longings of Christina Onassis.
With a weekly income of about $1 million dollars, she was
able to buy just about anything she wanted. When she was

living in Europe and wanted Diet Coke, which was available in the United States, she dispatched her private jet to buy a month's supply—it cost $30,000 per trip! She wanted twenty-four-hour companionship, so she sometimes offered friends $20,000 or $30,000 a month to stay with her. All her money didn't buy her happiness though. She died at thirty-seven of a heart attack that was likely brought on by repeated dieting bouts and her overuse of barbiturates.

Our treasures on earth can be used for eternity, however, and if we focus on God's Word and people's souls, those investments will last.

Father,
Thanks for reminders that all our earthly goods pass away. May our hearts be focused on what's lasting and eternal. Amen.

EXTRA READINGS FOR DAYS 6 AND 7
John 14:1-4; Revelation 22:1-5

[1]Jeanne Hendricks, *A Mother's Legacy* (Colorado Springs: NavPress, 1988), p. 110.

[2]Ellen Banks Elwell, *The Christian Mom's Idea Book* (Wheaton, Ill.: Crossway Books, 1997), p. 202.

[3]R. Kent Hughes, *James* (Wheaton, Ill.: Crossway Books, 1991), p. 267.

[4]Gladys Hunt, *Ms. Means Myself* (Grand Rapids, Mich.: Zondervan, 1972), p. 21.

[5]Kay Arthur, *To Know Him by Name* (Sisters, Ore.: Multnomah, 1995), p. 42.

[6]Susan Hunt, *The True Woman* (Wheaton, Ill. Crossway Books, 1997), p. 168.

[7]R. V. G. Tasker, *The General Epistle of James* (Grand Rapids, Mich.: Eerdmans, 1983), p. 93.

[8]R. Kent Hughes, *Hebrews* (Wheaton, Ill.: Crossway Books, 1993), p. 228.

[9]Quoted in James S. Hewett, *Illustrations Unlimited* (Wheaton, Ill.: Tyndale House, 1988), p. 256.

[10]Phillip W. Keller, *A Shepherd Looks at Psalm 23* (Grand Rapids, Mich.: Zondervan, 1970), p. 30.

[11]Bob Condor, "In Pursuit of Happiness," *Chicago Tribune*, December 10, 1998.

[12]"All Things in Jesus," *Worship and Service Hymnal* (Chicago: Hope Publishing Company, 1957), p. 290.

[13]James Houston, *The Heart's Desire* (Colorado Springs: NavPress, 1996), p. 97.

[14]"Not What These Hands Have Done," *The Worshiping Church Hymnal* (Carol Stream, Ill.: Hope Publishing Company, 1990), p. 476.

[15]Warren Wiersbe, *The Bible Exposition Commentary, Volume I* (Wheaton, Ill.: Victor Books, 1989), p. 68.

[16]William Neikirk, "To Repent: So Simple, Not So Easy," *Chicago Tribune*, August 30, 1998, Perspective, p. 1.

[17]*Chicago Tribune*, December 31, 1998, Section 5, p. 2.

[18]Lewis Smedes, *The Art of Forgiving* (New York: Ballantine, 1996), pp. 177-178.

[19]R. Kent Hughes, *1001 Great Stories and Quotes* (Wheaton, Ill.: Tyndale House, 1998), p. 304.

[20]*Worship and Service Hymnal* (Carol Stream, Ill.: Hope Publishing Company, 1957), p. 362.

[21]Adrian Rogers, *Believe in Miracles but Trust in Jesus* (Wheaton, Ill.: Crossway Books, 1997), pp. 104-105.

[22]Helen H. Lemmel, "Turn Your Eyes Upon Jesus," *The Worshiping Church Hymnal* (Carol Stream, Ill.: Hope Publishing Company, 1990), p. 452.

[23]R. Kent Hughes, *James* (Wheaton, Ill.: Crossway Books, 1991), p. 236.

[24]Ibid., p. 237.

[25]Randy Alcorn, *Money, Possessions and Eternity* (Wheaton, Ill.: Tyndale House, 1989), p. 175.

[26]Ibid., p. 151.